M

I'M NOT

Magical

MOMMY

I'M NOT

Magical

MOMMY

WHEN BEING A MOTHER JUST ISN'T ENOUGH,

TAKE TEN STEPS!

ANDREA GUICE

Print information available on the last page

Rev. date: 02/08/2018

Please go to www.imnotmagicalmommy.com for more
information about the book.

To order additional copies of this book, contact:
Xlibris
1-888-795-4274
www.Xlibris.com
Orders@Xlibris.com

TO MOTHERS AROUND THE WORLD

*The invisible bond of a mother to her child is like the air of life,
an invisible presence that exists, which no eye can describe.*
—Andrea Guice

CONTENTS

INTRODUCTION

What happens when a baby no longer needs the loving, tender nurture of their mommy? Let's look: breastfeeding during late nights, diaper changes, clothespins, bottles, formulas, many sleepless nights worrying about high fevers, visits to the doctor, potty training, teaching them to talk, wiping tears on their first day in kindergarten, musicals, sports, being a soccer mom, puppy love, dates, and driving lessons. Alas, that small baby has seemed to emerge into a full-blown teenager or has transcended into a young adult. Wait! It is no surprise your "big baby" is still so emotionally dependent on you. What does this all mean? What is a mother to do—next?

I am a mother of five children. I reflect on a time in my younger years when all I cared about was being a mom. I believed that being the perfect role model would make my children well-rounded and happy. I read many parenting books without realizing that there is no manual to teaching the most essential element of being a mom—love. Although I spent many years of stumbling through the maze of being the perfect mom—from movie tickets, sports games, school rehearsals, swimming lessons, music lessons, birthday parties, holiday celebrations, slumber parties, and toys galore—you name it, I did it! I fussed about messy rooms, personal sloppiness, and proper education, and boasted about how good I believed my children were. Sadly, deep inside, I knew they were not the perfect little angels that reading parenting books tends to convince parents they can become.

After years of jaunting through the task of being what I thought was the perfect family niche, my awakening surfaced because of an unfortunate divorce due to a dauntingly immature marriage, breaking the family foundation unwittingly and putting a damper on my children's outlook on life with saddened hearts. A broken home was never anything that I imagined and was the last thing I wanted my children to look forward to in their young lives. Ultimately, it was I—and not the other half of the family equation, their father—who took the brunt of the blame for the breakup of the family structure! Their father had little concern for the dismal outcome of a broken marriage with multiple children, and in the blink of an eye, he and his new woman moved forward without us in his life! I swallowed my pride. I decided to be true to my inner belief by keeping with good Christian values through attending church regularly. I believed that a proper mother who went to work each day and dedicated her life to the needs of her children would see those sacrifices in her children's future success. Looking back now, I was a single mom that didn't have a clue how to truly parent.

For the moms that have ever been through the wrenching heartbreak of a broken marriage, I went through all the tears and yells from the psychological pains of my kids' heartbreaking defeats. I bore the scars of whatever they felt was missing in their lives, which seemed to be their hopeless longing for their father's distant care and love. As the sole parent, I took on the reins of a dual role and began to wear many colorful jackets in the attempt to mend the broken dreams of my children. Alas, I became a "supermom," doing all I could to meet every single demand that my kids could extract for their joys. I realized later in life that there is no book that can teach you how to mend the broken dreams of a child or to help your child grow into their own potential of self-worth. It's a long journey of patience and understanding that comes through recognizing that love is the key through the lengthy process.

Time moved steadily forward, and my babies grew into young teens. I began to be dragged wearily into defeat by the impossible task of being the supermom! I became so disillusioned with being the perfect mom at all costs to satisfy only my children's longings. Until one spring day, while I was hurriedly cooking breakfast for my little darlings before dashing off to work, I began to question *why*. Why did I feel the urge to do what had become an impossible task—that being to please my children and do everything they thought I could? From every drama, any dilemma, a rebellious bull's-eye, every nuisance, and with heartbreaking guilt, I took it all without hesitation! Did I forget to mention I didn't look? I didn't! I had become robotic, putting hopeful aspirations on a shelf and becoming oblivious that all my intended goals had become stagnant. The fanciful dreams of becoming a model or singer and the even bigger thoughts of becoming a doctor were swept under the rug of realization that a regular job was front and center and a higher education was not in the equation.

This is what I believe many women who become moms do after they have children, with or without a husband or significant other. Women tend to halt their goals after they birth a child, and they allow their lives to become totally stagnant. This is the reason I decided to write this book. For all the mothers who have stopped looking at their dreams, for all the women who have put their aspirations on a shelf to collect dust and have fallen into the back seat of that wonderful ride of life, and who unconsciously veil any dreams for themselves—whether you are married, divorced, or single—this book is written for you with heartfelt emotions.

When you have given the best of yourself, knowing that you have made many sacrifices and that you have poured every ounce of your soul into your child's well-being, giving them the best of what you have—your heart—and then realizing your efforts don't seem to be enough, this book is meant for you and was written with you in mind. This book is about mothers who are beautiful human beings and who possess the indescribable magic of something we all know—that marvelous thing called motherly love.

Exploring these ten chapters is a basic guide to learning when being a mother doesn't feel enough. The *I'm Not Magical Mommy* book is written to remind us to "take ten steps and breathe in life." I hope these pages will encourage mothers and fathers who have been pushed to their boundaries of parenting to realize that being a magical mommy for their kids is impossible. If this is you or someone you know, it is time to return to your truth and reality. *You* are extraordinary!

Enjoy!

STEP 1

Breakfast

"What a wonderful morning," you say to yourself, looking up at the bright sun beaming warmth through the windowpane, as you turn to smack the alarm that woke you from your lovely beauty sleep. You stare blankly before the realization hits that you haven't cleaned the windows for months! "No matter," you tell yourself as you hastily move out of bed and grab that old bathrobe, stepping in time with the chugging of the gears in your head that beckon for its routine coffee. You know the morning routine blindfolded, and that brewed aroma you can smell tells you Mr. Caffeine is ready to be poured into your favorite cup. *Ah, my favorite flavor,* you think, having become accustomed to a delicious habit that helps the gears of a waking body move faster. After all, you must hurriedly cook breakfast for the kids or pour hot cereal into bowls those kids usually expect "Magical Mommy" to prepare.

Magical Mommy has been cooking for her children for years and has become their personal culinary chef—better than some that you have watched on marvelous TV chef shows! Above all, you have had fifteen years, or more, of daily cooking practice. *What a routine,* you think to yourself while heading to your kitchen to start cooking breakfast. You've managed to pour a second cup of your favorite concoction of caffeine and have chosen to quickly fry bacon and eggs, with the hopes that this will be a calmer morning and that your kids won't get upset with you for choosing to fix waffles instead of pancakes.

You reflect on the last outburst of anger from your children when they were not given what they expected for breakfast, never mind that you did your best to please them with a healthy meal. While grabbing the orange juice carton, you remember that you needed to buy orange juice the last time you had gone to the grocery store, and you swear while you shake the empty container. As always, one of the kids drank all but a drop and left the empty carton for you to discover in the refrigerator! Is this empty carton a kind reminder to buy more orange juice? You toss the empty container in the nearby trash, mumbling, *Why didn't the child who drank the last bit of juice mention it while I was grocery shopping?* You heave a sigh, with a mind now racing and hands that seem to move like octopus arms, moving frantically about, trying to get everything prepared on time so that your kids won't have to wait or complain! After all, they are growing up and they need a nutritious diet to develop healthy bodies, a wholesome meal that you readily provide.

As your mind is racing to get them breakfast, you can hear their groans and fussiness. "I'm hungry," says a voice. "Going as fast as I can," you quip. "I want it now," says a demanding tone. You glance toward the direction of a sleepy face with eyes partially opened, which seem to pierce through you. You predict the onslaught of complaints, as always! "The eggs aren't done enough," "The toast isn't hot enough," "The butter isn't melted," and "It's not pancakes!" "This is wrong" or "That is wrong," and never a "Thank you, Mom" or "Great breakfast, Mom." You feel like you're standing on pins and needles while you suck in your anxiousness and gulp your coffee, which is now lukewarm. You steadily watch a ticking clock on the wall that tells you that your kids need to be at school on time and that you need to leave for work and cannot be late! When duties of parents are essential to the development of children and when the management of time for rigorous schedules associated with home life must be met, what does a mommy do? Where does the line get drawn for effective parenting during the juggle between jobs and family?

Parents are not magical, and they cannot make their children smile every second of every hour. Most parents spend twenty-four hours a day taking care of their children's wants and ensuring that their children are provided with the necessary support they need. When parenting does become apparently dramatic, as seen in the breakfast scenario above, certain precautions should be taken to prevent a parent from becoming overly stressed. Some parents that are ill-adapted to managing family schedules, juggling between their children's needs and their jobs or educational careers or other family matters, can begin to feel ineffective with the parenting role. A parent that is overburdened can begin to show negative behavior patterns—drinking, smoking, drug use, or other more serious problems—which can be the result of what is termed a burnout or medical depression.

When parenting begins to show obvious signs of uncontrolled stress, the usual pattern that can develop is a dysfunction of the family. The dysfunctional behavior by parents in the home, which could be life-threatening, displayed by an adult or a child, must be stopped right away by professional intervention from a health professional, or in extreme cases, from law enforcement. There is medical literature on depression disorders and many community health outreach programs for anyone that needs support to cope with family problems. (See "Magical Mommy Resource Guide.")

Here is the clue:

The start for making the necessary adjustments to manage your family schedules sufficiently is to first save your strength. The days of breastfeeding are done, and your child has passed the stage of infancy. Most children have the intelligence to prepare food for themselves, but they must be taught good eating habits. When you recognize that your child has reached a level of competency in which they no longer need Mommy to feed, clothe, or bathe them, it is time to teach them more self-reliance.

Teaching children they are capable of fixing their own breakfast can begin with stocking up on several boxes of their favorite cereal and buying plenty of milk! It is time to change the constant morning dramas of the children's complaints, which will only worsen if not properly managed. Parents owe themselves time alone without the hassles of dramatic home atmospheres. A relaxed family environment will reduce stress loads for the kids and parents. With extra time, parents can enjoy relaxation or pursue a hobby or have a sense of well-being to give their child's needs.

By teaching your children simple steps to be responsible, morning breakfast can be less hectic, and Magical Mommy can use the extra morning time at a slower pace—while drinking her *favorite* coffee before tackling job obligations. Teaching children to accept doing a task can take time before the benefit is seen or appreciated by both parent and child. This could be teaching children to do early morning chores such as making their beds or taking out trash or shoveling snow.

Parents who are prudent with managing time can be at ease and can enjoy mornings without the anxiety from dissatisfied kids that have outgrown Magical Mommy Chef. The management of schedules is not limited to breakfast mornings, but it is necessary to manage a family's home-life entirely. Remember, there are twenty-four hours in a day! Being capable of juggling kids, work, education, and other duties is a lifelong task.

The clue is simple: Manage time wisely. Help children understand responsibility. Instruct your children how to do basic tasks for themselves. When a child stubbornly refuses to accept the instructions given by an adult, this is a telltale sign of up-and-coming problems. (Children with temperament issues are covered in chapter 6.) In any case, teaching children new responsibilities will require time and patience. If a child refuses to cooperate with parents when other duties are introduced, do not fret or become angry. Parents should not ignore teaching a child work ethic that will be useful to them later or succumb to a child's obstinate refusal to respect your wishes. Many kids will use tears or other obnoxious means to avoid doing some specific chore requested by their parent. Explain to them that you must keep a job schedule to provide the necessities they need and the things they want, such as a new computer game or other stuff they enjoy, and that pitching in to help Mommy makes a difference. It's teamwork. (Concerned dads can help too!)

There comes a time when your child must realize how to service themselves and realize that they can learn to do many tasks at home without whining for Mommy to get things done for them. It is time for both Magical Mommy and her children to learn techniques that will help the entire family. Learning is an integral part of life experience. The learning process begins at birth and continues throughout a child's development and throughout the parenting role. There will be new techniques for parents to teach and for children to learn. Breakfasts can be delightful memories.

The greatest teacher is not magic, but the test of skills from Magical Mommy's time.

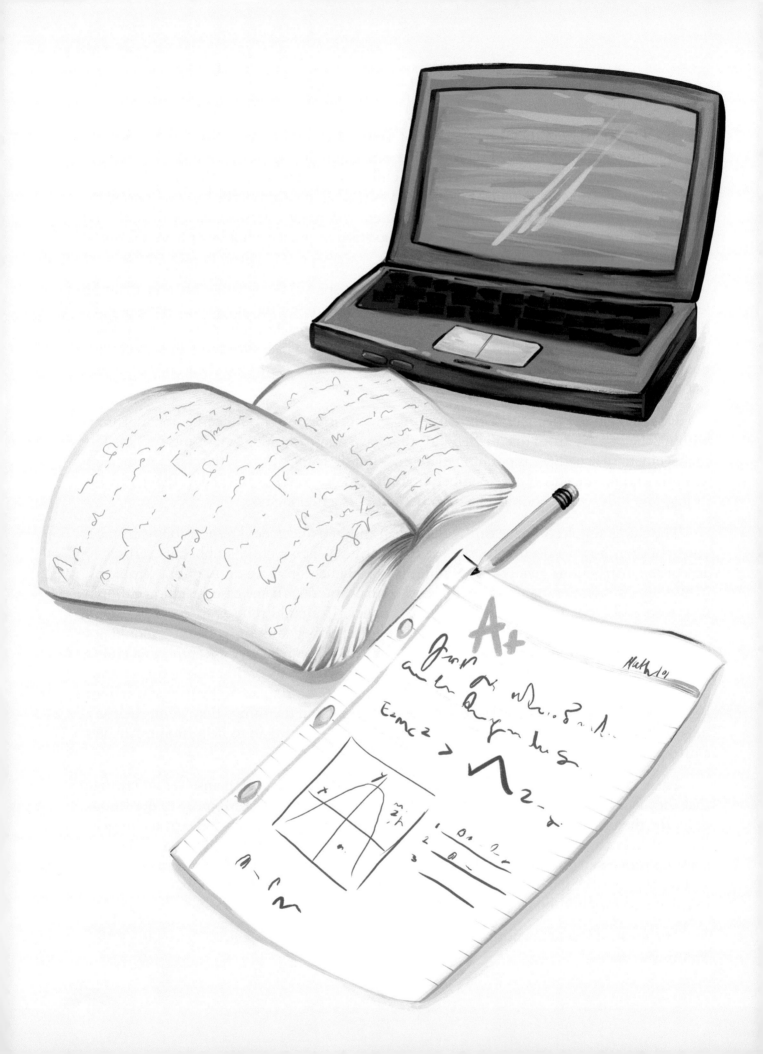

STEP II
School and Homework

For all that life is worth, a magical mommy deserves a medal for the devotion she gives to her child from birth. Magical Mommy relentlessly spends time caring for her children's lives, from soccer games, hockey, football, basketball, to fund-raisers, musical recitals, camping trips, open houses—the list goes on and on, all the way up to the graduation ball! And let's not forget nail-biting prom night! We moms are truly magical! Yet, for all the time and effort we devote to our youngsters up to their adulthood, those young folk we call ours do not truly recognize the constant efforts of our being their parents—particularly single moms—and they often ignore the signs of their own adolescent hurdles, which are commonly known as growing pains.

There are children or teenagers or young adults that do not consider the time or money that is needed for dining out (pizza fun), sports, house parties, and social events that have turned Mom into "Soccer Mom," a superhero! She transports her kids to every sporting event or other activities, juggling the minutes, hours, and days of her time year after year. Magical Mommy never asks for anything in return, other than for her darling children to put their best foot forward, who are generally brooding . . . for more of her time! Tsk, tsk!

Oh, never mind that Magical Mommy is painstakingly guiding and encouraging her children by giving them valuable lessons on maturity and responsibility, that they can feel prided from her diligence of being a positive role model. Never mind that she is someone with strong work ethics and strategies for obtaining a firm education and who has hope that her children will carry the torch of success to become fine citizens within society. However, disappointments can happen.

Many children do not own the skills of diplomacy or tactfulness and have the tendency to be brutally honest and dreadfully disrespectful. The children's lack of cooperation is socially apparent in today's ever-mounting parental challenges. It is unfortunate that some kids are not restricted early to curtail habits that can be harmful to themselves or others, and sadly, children who become independent can adopt ill-mannered behavior unsuited for interacting socially. This type of family dysfunction can cause *poor* mommy to constantly panic and become worrisome, which is cause for more dismay and lack of healthy communication between a mother and her child.

When communication leans toward constantly nagging your child, "Hurry for school or you will be late" or "Do your homework" or "Do not play computer games" or "No, friends cannot visit," this may be a signal that your child is showing a behavior of rebellion. This may be in the form of pouts or other unfavorable attitude, ignoring Mommy altogether by grumps and slumps on a comfortable couch while watching their favorite TV programs or playing video games, or yelling at Mommy. Typically, children's tirades of "What's for dinner? I'm hungry" or their fits of rage by slamming doors or their sneaking friends into the home when parents aren't around is a red flag for ill-mannered behavior that reveals appropriate disciplinary action is needed.

Parents should recognize when to stop a child's rude behavior; if left unchecked, it can result to incorrigible behavior that is manifested in their adulthood. Diligence and wise actions are key for children who display rudeness; they must be corrected with proper discipline. Unfortunately, young children generally do not have a clue how far they push the boundaries of expectation, wanting Magical Mommy to wait on them hand and foot and to attend to their every demand. The unrealistic expectations parents try to fulfill for disrespectful kids can be exhausting. A parent needs to recognize when to stop bowing to their child's bidding, in which Mommy has now become more like a maidservant to them instead of a mother. It is time to open your eyes, Magical Mommy, and see that a behavior change needs to start now!

Here is the clue:

Magical Mommy calmly turns off the TV, video games, and cell phones, and firmly directs those children to get their school books and start homework, now! And there will be no meals until the homework is done! It is time for Magical Mommy to take back control of who she is! That is, she is not her children's servant, nor is she the chauffeur or personal chef! It is time for Mommy to realize that there is a time when we all must become responsible for the actions of choice, and those kids need to learn it by respecting authority—hers!

Magical Mommy needs to realize that she must not enable unruly behavior from her children and that it is time for her to take control of the onslaught of dizzying madness. As the old saying goes, "People will only do what you allow them to," and that logic also applies to children. Children will do what parents allow them to do, and it is imperative for parents to understand that they have a responsibility to teach their children good and moral principles.

Parenting is not easy. It's also not magic! When Mommy takes a firm hold of controlling the family situation and the fairy-dust mind-set of the children settles, knowing Mom has had enough disrespect and that they must respect her authority, she can finally kick her heels up and relax. After having gained the control of the family issues in a positive manner, you can feel the accomplishment upon seeing your children respectfully and independently doing the chores and their schoolwork, which was long overdue! This is the correct way for Magical Mommy to gain control of parenting.

Magical Mommy must build her own self-worth by teaching her children to be respectful of her and to respect authority from other adults, particularly teachers that provide educational instructions to those kids for a much-needed higher education. Teach your child to understand that respect brings positive results and that respecting you also gives the right kind of balance for the family structure to be a comfortable and peaceful home. With respect, there will be a suitable environment that will provide children with a sense of pride to be productive and responsible.

Providing children with meaningful instructions toward responsibility—which will afford them the wisdom to control their own actions—should encourage a positive outlook that can result to greater satisfaction in their future endeavors, which can lead to the continuation of a higher education toward college. I call this RTTA (response to their ability)! Magical Mommy is now in control and can rest assured that her children know that the rules must be adhered to, to achieve their intended future goals. Time to relax, Magical Mommy, because you deserve it!

STEP III
Friendships and Relationships

Life is full of emotions, and all humans share the need for companionship, no matter the age. From the nurturing of infancy and growing past toddler days into the curiosity of youth, there will appear new reckonings for your children. The time will come that your young man or little lady begins to feel they want—or need—to have their own friends or relationships with someone other than their mommy. It's okay to feel emotional! Take a breath, because that's what growing up is all about!

However, there are a few rules to the friendship game. Let's begin by evaluating some of these thought-provoking rules. Female adolescents will ultimately become women. Young girls must accept the fact of being a female, and in society today, peer pressure can be challenging. Learning to accept flaws based on what is considered the norm is impractical. Here is where Mommy can give the truth serum of reality by telling her child that there is no perfect person. Makeup can hide some facial flaws, and diet fads can be harmful; however, your child must accept themselves for the good, the bad, and the imperfections. (Perfect is flawed!)

Your child may be measuring their self-worth based on misguided information from many sources—TV, social media, ads, and peer pressure. You're probably asking what I am talking about here. Well, let's examine some of the facts. There are so many delicate issues for young females to contend with. From unwanted facial pimples to the onset of menstrual cycles (which is Mother Nature's female eye-opener), feminine mood swings and bouts of uncontrollable tears, and doubts relating to self-esteem may surface, which is common among young females who enter this stage of puberty. It's quite normal! However, it may feel the reverse very much . . . every month!

Your daughter may display many teary-eyed outbursts with a barrage of kaleidoscope personalities that may make you feel a sense of helplessness, which you or your child is unable to manage with tactfulness. Patience is truly the key in this phase of your child's delicate growth process. Remember, you are her mother, and you share the awareness of being a female. Moms know firsthand the female journey that brings the burden of menstrual cycle symptoms inherently had by almost all females who transcend into womanhood. This is the time when Mommy's understanding ought to present itself with an insight for much needed maturity by giving the utmost support to aid her daughter's physical transformation. Magical Mommy's knack for showing patience and loving calmness under pressure can help her daughter cope at this time of her physical development. Take a deep breath!

A mother's knowledge that her young daughter's anatomical growth will need extra care to be dealt with is a major responsibility for both. Your child will be faced with a major life-altering condition that needs sensible and considerate support. You could go on an occasional shopping spree or a getaway excursion out of town together, or you could dine out at her favorite restaurant to curb some sad feelings and mood swings that are associated with the common symptoms of an altering *female* body. As a woman, the reflection back into time when these unavoidable bodily changes occurred brings tears, even now! You can remember experiencing similar feelings of discomfort with the arrival of a menstrual cycle. You recognize the uneasiness from firsthand experience, and you know at this juncture that your child will need increased allowances, medicines, extra bed rest, or in extreme cases, a doctor's visit. Explain to your daughter that the menstrual cycle is a regular, natural change that occurs in the female reproductive system; the personal responsibility of a young female's menstrual periods demands a detailed discussion.

Mothers know well by subjective experience that female life can be straining, particularly by a younger female's lack of knowledge on how to manage her physical growth. Life for females can be overwhelming, and this is the time to really flex the Magical Mommy muscles. I know, I know . . . the book is *I'm Not Magical Mommy*. However, females know that this is the absolute exception! (Sniffle.) With your wise guidance, your little lady can eventually learn to juggle her life with better understanding on how to handle personal requirements.

There will be a time when the word *drama* can take on a new meaning when it comes to the role of parenting. Your child, male or female, will want to venture into unknown territory upon entering the puberty stage of their life. With every phase of adolescence into adulthood, there will be new responsibilities, and the choices will mount for young adults. One such choice may bring on the want of your child to follow the in crowd. Without good parental guidance, the choice to follow a popular peer group can result in an overpowering dilemma. *OMG!* you say. Yes! Whether your child is a gal or a guy, the importance of this particular topic of how your child picks their friends must be considered very carefully.

All kids choose their own friends, and sometimes the friends they do choose are not good influences. You acknowledge that not everyone is a good influence, but to convey that message to your child can bring on feelings of resentment. Parents know the importance for adolescents to avoid peers who show unethical behavior, which unfortunately beguile the best intentions immature children have, and who tend to sway in the wrong direction if not watched. Parents that allow their children to engage into friendships with the wrong types of influences will be enabling an ill-fated future. Mommy should carefully check the choice of companions that her child associates with, and she should set the ground rules of expectations.

Many teens view hanging out after school or after curfews as cool. These are just a few no-nos that need to be discussed with your child. There are some establishments that view groups of kids hanging out as troublesome, and merely a bystander's anonymous call to law enforcement can pose major problems for your child. To prevent your child from becoming involved with infractions with the law, loitering, or being involved with gangs that could be an even greater risk, a parent's responsibility requires an active role that does not halt because your child has entered their teenage phase. It is crucial to take any action to protect your child from making mistakes that they may later regret. Take it slow, but be diligent.

You have been your child's parent for a long time and want to keep the proper rapport with your child. Nevertheless, as your child's parent, you should exercise proper authority. Schedule a time that you can discuss with your child the importance of social relationships and what you believe good friendship should be or should not be. Remain open-minded to your child's opinions about what they perceive are good relationships or friendships. The reality is that parents want their children to be happy with their friendships and relationships and, ultimately, for them not to dive into anything that will result in hurt and sadness.

Parents do not want their kids to step into social situations that can involve bad influences that later could be detrimental to their well-being. It is likely that any negative influences could result in you having to endure the brunt of possible serious problems when your youngster cannot decide what or what not to follow, or whom or whom not to follow. The societal trends are unbelievably abundant! From those short daisy duke skirts and shorts to trousers and pants hanging obnoxiously lower than diapers, which your child believes is perfectly acceptable to imitate, Mommy must set the standards.

Do not faint just yet! Did you buy the cell phone that your kid spends hours upon hours on, chatting and texting while oblivious to the world? (Oh, the cost of that bill!) These are just a few of the telltale signs for you to take the proper steps necessary (never mind the constant tears or tantrums . . . I will cover that in the next chapter) to curtail negative influences that your child could become involved with. I call this an NITB (nip in the bud).

Help your children understand the pros and cons of following other people's ideas or trends, as opposed to being an independent thinker, who can make standalone decisions without outsider coercions. Teach your child that trending has its place and that bad trends will not improve their growth and will not bring happy, successful friendships and relationships in the long run. There will be those times your youngster will demand to see a certain boy or girl whom Mommy perceives to be unsuitable company—repeat, *following strangers is not a wise choice!* That is when Magical Mommy must be strong enough to handle the challenge with wisdom by simply telling her child the magic word—*no*!

Parents need to commit to the rules that they set for their kids. Sticking to the rules with firm commitment ensures the best outcome for your child while they are creating their identity. Supporting kids' self-esteem can help them to avoid the tragedies that are often associated with young people's inability to choose correct paths to follow in life. There are many situations that occur because of a youngster's self-doubts and his or her inability to move beyond irrational thoughts. The profound consequences that can happen when a child is plagued by self-uncertainty can lead to irrational ideas or behavior, for which many teen pregnancies have been a common result.

You may remember when you were a young adult and had questionable friends that you, too, may have been adamant about keeping, and your mother or father promptly stepped in to referee your choices. You may have felt that your parents were unfair to negatively criticize that guy with the unkempt hair or that girlfriend whose grades were Fs or that friend with awful hygiene; you may have stubbornly refused to agree with your parents about these issues. It may awaken past sensitivities when you look back in the history of your adolescence that had many challenges, yet successfully reared you into an adult. You can feel good knowing that you had the guidance and intervention caring parents. (Hands are folded!)

Thank heavens you realized that your own parents cared enough to give intelligent guidance that prevented you from making wrong choices, and those wise parental instructions have been passed on to you! You realize your parents were not magicians, and though they were not, they always protected you and saw your best potential, even when you did not know how to choose the best course to take for yourself. Your parents were wise and ever had you in their hearts. Magical Mommy has her children in her heart too, and grandparents cherish their marvelous grandchildren.

When parents' strategies to stop a child's undesirable behavior fails, with ground rules broken and advice completely ignored, it is a sign to obtain professional help that will intervene against your child's destructive behavior. There are various organizations that offer counseling for adolescent conduct and behavioral problems. This may be a final solution for parents to help their child control the behavior problems during a critical point in their life. Effective intervention strategies for behavior difficulties can give your child the tools needed to decrease problems and teach methods that can help them make better choices for becoming stable adults.

Here is the clue:

The following are a few signs that your children may be in serious need of your Magical Mommy guidance and behavior intervention: disrespecting parents, aggression, trouble behaving in school, withdrawal and unresponsiveness, using inappropriate or harassing language, hanging out later than usual, and bad associations. Today's society has shown that teen drug usage is no secret. With the technology of cell phones, social media, and many sites that offer teens pleasure and social fulfillment, parents must keep a close eye on their child's daily routine. Maladaptive behavioral changes may show that your child is having a psychological meltdown that will need immediate action. It is no secret that on the internet many youths are befriended by absolute strangers who could lure them into a dangerous situation, and abnormal behavior patterns could be the only noticeable clue.

I think that parents want their kids to know they trust them, and they don't want to be a sneak when it comes to their children's personal preferences. After all, parents teach their kids to be independent, and that comes with trusting them to make decisions. Even so, young minds aren't actually equipped with the experience to know when they are headed toward a path of ruin, such as drug usage or meeting a dangerous stranger on an internet site. When those aforementioned dangers occur within a family, it needs early action for the children's safety.

There are also laws that prohibit certain websites for adolescents. You won't regret interfering or using restrictions to enforce the abuse of internet usage, as these may be your only means to ensure the protection of your children, who may not realize the dangers they could be headed toward. A parent's role is to responsibly take the steps necessary to prevent danger to their child when troubled behavior becomes obvious. Your children depend on you for so much, and this is one time you can make a Magical Mommy difference. They too will fold their hands with gratitude. You can seek more information on professional intervention regarding substance abuse in the resource guide at the end of this book.

STEP IV
Tantrums

The whys of what are known as tantrums have been studied by psychologists, and many books have been written with theories for children that display temper tantrums. There are many parents that have experienced their children displaying emotional outbursts when they are unable to do what they want. The parents' failed attempts to manage their youngster's angry behavior can result in a child's stubborn defiance or, in turn, result in a hissy fit! The emotional meltdown shown by some children may leave a parent with little sway to stop their child's inflated self-image. How is a mommy to handle a child that is showing these types of tirades?

The remembrance of your endearing crying infant has now faded into a screaming toddler or adolescent. The helpless baby sounds are a far cry (excuse the pun) from the screaming and yelling, or even hitting, that you will hear from your children as they start growing into young men and women who have not outgrown temper tantrums. Get ready and hold on to your sanity! There may come a time when you will need to count to ten before exploding over the constant barrage of child tantrums. Remember, Mommy must remain calm in her child's storms. Count *one, two, three,* and wisdom beckons to choose time-out rather than entering a mommy moment outrage, or what I call an MMO!

Let's examine what Mommy should do about keeping her composure when her youngster has become seemingly unreasonable with their demands. A scenario unfolds like this: The child has been told no about something that they want Mommy to provide. The child becomes disagreeable and shows agitation with angry ranting meant to control Mommy. The child's anger may be in the form of crying, throwing things, stomping, holding their breath, hitting, and yelling at Mommy. A mommy may apply pacification attempts (cuddling) to calm the child, although these attempts rarely satisfy the child's reluctance of not being given what they wish.

A second scenario unfolds like this: The child has been told no about something they wish. The child reacts by having a temper tantrum that may result in the parent responding in like manner, that being an adult tirade against the child—yelling, scolding, or spanking the child with the intent to control them in public or at home, with little results. Although children's tantrums can be distressing to a parent, the reasonable method of handling children with tantrum problems is firstly for Mommy to keep herself calm. There are strategies galore that have been written by experts to help de-escalate children's tantrums. No, it's not abracadabra, Magical Mommy!

At some point from infancy to being toddlers, generally ages one to four, a parent's ability to effectively communicate becomes lost. A newborn baby must adapt to the weaning process, and the withdrawal from the bond of an infant born from a mother is significant to rearing a child. This process differs for each parent-child bond. There are also cultural differences that can create a distinct set of ideas of how children are nurtured and weaned. Is there an actual time frame to wean a baby from its mother? And is there any adverse effect after weaning a baby from its natural bond with its mother that could be a factor for later tantrums?

In today's society, there are many working women that have busy schedules and do not have the luxury of nurturing a baby past a few months. Pediatricians suggest a minimum of six months for a mother to nurture a newborn baby. This is often impossible for many women who are employed by employers that have no allowances for a lengthy maternity leave. There will be many challenges for a new mother to find the right balance to nurture, wean, and withdraw naturally from a growing baby; ignoring the sensitivities of the weaning process altogether can also be a factor for the emerging development of ill-tempered children that eventually display temper tantrums. Remember, you are not magical, but you are the adult that is serving the emotional and physical needs of your child. There will be a lengthy growth process for the child that a parent will need to understand.

You may have several children, but each child is uniquely different. Mommy must put aside any comparison with other siblings and recognize the individuality of her children. As children grow into their own identity, a parent's interaction with one child can easily cause a sibling rivalry or jealousy with another child. Parents must take care to understand the dissimilar needs of each one of her children to avoid spats and rivalry, as these types of situations can trigger many childhood resentments that may manifest into bullying. Mommy needs to take the initiative to know the relevance in staying in control and to give the correct guidance to her children.

There may be situations that call for expert evaluation when the child has passed toddler stages and is into adolescence with a temper tantrum problem. An adolescent child who displays resistance to a parent's attempts at reasoning by blowing up and who shows such illogical anger through violent speech or even by striking a parent needs medical help. Mommy must muster her courage and obtain immediate intervention to correct this type of out-of-norm behavior.

You don't have to engage in the fight-or-fright with your child! Let your youngster blow their horn of perceived injustices—or bubbles, for that matter—but when any child begins to project violent tendencies toward a parent, it is time to act quickly and responsibly and deflate it! After the rantings and ravings of these child tantrums, or cat-and-mouse (which one are you, hmmm?) standoffs, it is time for Magical Mommy to come up for air, staying above the fragility of weariness from weeks of your child's unyielding emotions. Once the storms of your child's tantrums have passed and are understood, either by medical evaluation or other means, you will have become a stronger and wiser mommy!

There are many methods of helping your child control the feelings that trigger anger and lead to emotional outbursts. About now, you may be asking, *how do you gain control of an out-of-control child?* First, sit down with your child when they have become calm. Tell your child that you would like them to write down how they feel on a piece of paper. This method is one of many therapeutic strategies that may teach your child to recognize how to cope with their anger. Parents that have toddlers can try other simpler methods, like coloring or digital learning tools. This positive technique is meant to help your youngsters become aware of their positive feelings that include the attention of their parent. As you apply various techniques to children that show them skills to restrain angry outbursts, your youngster will learn to become less resistant and are much happier.

When confronting an adolescent, approach the situation after they have quieted down. Begin by telling your youngster that you won't tolerate being yelled at or other intolerable behavior. Mommy should keep a journal to monitor how she is handling the situation too. Yes, you too! Mommies are not made of stone! Mommies have feelings too! During times when your child is calm, fixing a cup of tea or hot chocolate to sip together at a table or watching a favorite TV show can provide an atmosphere of balance and calmness, and that will create positive feelings that may rekindle trust to communicate more effectively.

There may be such tension that you feel the need to go to a different part of the home to diffuse. However, do not alienate, disassociate, or ignore the problems. Remember, problems don't go away; they can just fester and grow until there seems to be an *eight-hundred-pound gorilla* in the room. Let's hope not! (Sigh!) Mommy, you may want to wait several hours or even a couple of days to let your feelings become calm and diffused before sitting down with your youngster for a powwow, a meeting between you and them.

Having paper and pen, inform your young man or young lady to bring their paper on which they are to write down their feelings, and calmly begin to discuss the issues. It may be tough to open, but this is the time to air out any hurtful feelings and return to a sense of normalcy. You will need to fully explain to your youngster what you expect from them (depending on the age of a child), that it is time for them to change those tantrums, and that their disruptive behavior is unacceptable. It is your responsibility to recognize your child's changed disposition, and laying down the ground rules provides a remedy that they can follow to prevent the unwanted tantrums. If the tantrums persist and cannot be successfully eliminated by warnings, time-outs, or sensible methods, it is a cue to consult an expert. More information can be found in the "Magical Mommy Resource Guide" at the end of this book.

Find a qualified counselor to help your child when you recognize that more intervention is needed, but under no circumstances should you harshly punish your child or ignore serious behavior problems your child is experiencing. You're not Magical Mommy but a person with a youngster that needs support for social development. You need to provide the necessary means for your child to learn self-discipline and for you to have a healthy home environment. It can be successfully achieved with patience and consistency.

Here is the clue:

Avoid a head-on collision between you and your child's feelings. No combat! Stay calm under pressure and don't engage in the angered youngster's behavior. Wait, defuse, and show them respect. This strategy can ultimately teach them to be more relaxed with you, knowing you will not or cannot be persuaded by their screaming, throwing objects, hitting, or other inappropriate actions they direct toward you. A mother is not a magician that can miraculously cure all the psychological difficulties during a child's development.

When family situations become obviously out of control because of unruly kids, it is a parent's duty to tackle their youngster's behavioral issues. Doing so needs maturity and the ability to know the various methods that will create the necessary changes. Arguing with your youngster will bring resentment. Most of the time, a carefully thought-out plan to help your child's tantrums will need every ounce of a parent's patience. Remember, your youngster is growing up and needs your presence of stability. It's up to parents to set the example.

It has been a long road to this point, possibly without a father. Recognize that kids have tantrums to express their inability to communicate what is bothering them or causing them hurt. This can be in the form of mental or physical problems due to causations known or unknown, which they cannot express other than with emotional outbursts and which they feel uncomfortable or afraid or incapable to talk about with their parent. Most parents can sense when there is something seriously wrong with their child.

A parent and a child are connected in a miraculous journey of give and take, but children need an abundant amount of encouragement by their parents' support while they advance through the developmental process to becoming an adult. There is no magic mommy formula! A parent needs to stay coolheaded under pressure. Quite simply, the magic is a mother's knowing patience.

STEP V
Guilt Jackets

How many jackets can one wear at a time? This is the ultimate test for Magical Mommy! Let's examine the meaning for *guilt*. There are many theories written by trained experts who have studied the human rationale for standards of conduct that are associated with guilty feelings. Though no theory is precise, the subject of guilt is still a major study in the field of psychology and psychiatry. Principal factors must be viewed for the causes associated with the human struggle between the unconscious forces within an individual that contribute to guilt, which is recognized in the medical community to be an illness.

How does guilt begin, and whom does it affect? The answer is "anytime and anyone." But this is not a psychology course; let's review a few basics from parents embedded with the duties of parenthood. Beginning with the newborn baby, there is a term for mothers called *postpartum depression*. This label was given to women by doctors that viewed the end of a pregnancy to cause psychological changes to women in forms of depression.

It is not unusual for a woman to have children without the support of a loving spouse or a young female to become pregnant without proper understanding about responsibilities associated with an unwanted pregnancy. Many females will show signs of depression after having given birth to her child. There can be many scenarios: An unmarried (or married) man or young boy who has regrettably received information that a female is pregnant and bearing his seed can refuse to accept responsibility of the impregnation or the fact of the child being theirs altogether. There could be legal circumstances that can be another contributing factor to the postpartum depression. These themes will vary in many cases but ultimately can and do affect the mind-set of a female after she has birthed a baby.

With these issues of unwanted pregnancies, there are many couples that want children but are saddened by the inability to bear a child, and these unrecognized feelings can set the stage for guilt or shame. A good case in point is that a couple may have to reevaluate buying a home or put plans of vacations on hold or even choose to forgo a college dream. For couples that cannot achieve having a baby, or have problems with infertility, the many trips to a medical doctor may be a financial burden and can be disheartening. Be that as it may, there are many relationships that produce children, ready or not! Quite obviously! Mommy will be faced with the greater responsibility, from the nine months of pregnancy, to birth and eighteen long years thereafter. Teary-eyed yet? You are not alone!

How parents adjust to parenthood affects children. Your child will need constant attention from the time he or she is born. When the infancy phase moves into the toddler stage, it may not be an easy transition for the child or the parent. Oh, the tears! This is normal. Children need and yearn for plenty of attention—generally, yours! Magical Mommy's attention will become her child's security blanket, and in turn, a mommy will be their child's *security* jacket! Let's view jacket 1. As time pushes forward while Mommy cares for a newborn baby, routines tend to inadvertently become jackets. The process for nurturing Mom's little bundle of newborn joy—breastfeeding, formulas, changing diapers, sleepless nights, and visits to the doctor—rolls into the toddler years. How time flies! As a baby grows into a toddler, many parents often cling to jacket 1! The toddler becomes aware of his or her abilities through motor skills—responding to sounds, sitting alone, teething, standing, grasping objects, recognizing simple words, crawling, climbing up stairs and furniture, and much more—by way of emotional and social development. Parents can feel a heavier burden during the developmental period of their toddler. Your toddler's increased child development will ease (hopefully smoothly!) into comprehensive skills that will prepare them for the next phase of their growth, adolescence, and it is the signal that parents need to remove jacket 1.

Mommies can oftentimes be reluctant to stop spoiling their child during the adolescent stage. It is normal for parents to feel the need to protect their children. This is when painful denial can come to light by a mommy's unacceptance of her baby outgrowing the close bond that they had with her. This is when the feelings of guilt can appear. It is a delicate balance for any parent to resist coddling, pampering, or spoiling their baby; however, overprotective parenting can give your child a false sense of entitlement that can create a spoiled brat. There comes a time when Magical Mommy must realize that time doesn't wait, that change is imminent, and that your child needs a parent who recognizes their responsibility to use sensible reassurances without excessive mollycoddling. The demands from that adored baby that you fussed over night and day are gone, and you acknowledge he or she has morphed into adolescence. You wish they could have stayed your little baby forever. You are mesmerized at how fast your sweet angel grew. "Where did the time go?" You sigh.

The day will come when jacket 1 feels uncomfortable as your child reaches that threshold of adolescence phase of their development. At this point, parents may notice that the child's behavior has a spellbinding dual role. It may seem like Mommy has now become the child and the child has become the mommy! (Did you overindulge in spoiling? Oh dear!) During adolescence, there may be yells of "Why?" no matter the situation! The continued "Why not? Why can't I?" or even "I hate you" may be some comments your adolescent shouts at you. Have you gone into disbelief yet? You perhaps may think, "It's all my fault," or if you're a single mom, you may blame yourself for the failure of your marriage (or relationship), for why your child is demanding or seemingly angry in his or her adolescence. At this stage of parenthood, many parents can feel that they are in a losing battle with their child. The feelings of guilt may seem colossal! Don't fret! It's time for Mommy to realize that she needs another jacket. I call this jacket 2.

Your heart was so happy when that baby arrived that you didn't think about the many changes that would later appear . . . like magic! It was not magic, but it is your child's individuality! The adolescent years of your child have caught you totally by surprise, and you feel the uneasiness of that transition into jacket 2. What is a mother to do with a yelling and demanding adolescent child? Enter the twilight zone of your child's unique personality, their adolescence unlike any other. (No comparisons!) Mommy, if you can make it through your child's adolescence, you deserve a medal; you may be swooning with doubt, but don't give up before your child reaches adulthood at age eighteen. Magical Mommy, just hold on to your sanity! Your child is no longer interested in cuddling or baby talk, although they may expect to be spoiled rotten. Those days are long gone!

The shift into reckoning that you are dealing with an emerging young adult is challenging. The question of *who the mommy is* may pop into your mind while you're reeling from how you became second in your adolescent child's self-centered bubble. There is an old saying: "The world is a stage, and everyone plays a part." It seems that the part you've begun to play is a shadowy stranger in a fiction novel, written by the cleverness of your adolescent youngster. Yes, Magical Mommy, kids are very smart, and they have been watching you from that first moment they arrived.

There will be ruminations while jacket 2 is worn. This is the time to recognize that your child's development is either good or bad. Parents need to use reasonable authority to put a stop to their child's unhealthy habits. Magical Mommy, this is the time to step into the full gear of jacket 2. It is time to discard the negative demands of your *adorable* adolescent child. Know that the growth phases in children have always been weighed by parents' strengths or weaknesses. It is time that Mommy shift into Magical Mommy gear to face the challenges of her child's pivotal time in life—growing up. No more yells or discontented attitudes that force Mommy to become guilty will be tolerated. No more pouts and meltdowns in public that cause onlookers to gawk as if Mommy is inept at controlling her child. Guilt stops now! It is about time to change jacket 2, *not into a straitjacket!*

There will be days that you will wish you were magical, to be able to snap a finger, to make all the challenges of parenting disappear. Guilt feelings about being inadequate may occur when the mind cannot get a grip of normalcy due to undue pressures. A mother is a biological being with human mechanics that includes the reproductive system, with innumerable patterns for the child bonding process that seems to differ for everyone.

The anxiety that a mother can experience during child-rearing is a psychological defense mechanism that can be overcome by knowing that no one can truly judge you except you. Magical Mommy, it is time to remove doubts about your ability and realize that you are a caring parent. It is time for the change to jacket 3!

Proper discipline will help your child's transition into his or her teenage stage of life. Parents need to provide a safe and meaningful home but avoid unstructured and chaotic environments that are detrimental to a child's health. Begin with scheduling everything, from breakfast, lunch, dinner, to school, playtime, and discipline. Parents need to teach their children to follow basic routines that will provide constructive habits. Effective parenting involves wearing many hats; there is nothing set in stone for teaching the right methods. Parenting needs a steady balance. What may be a solution for one situation involving a child may not be the suitable approach for another child. There is no one-size-fits-all-children solution.

There will be times when Mommy may need to apply restrictions on her child. There are many discipline techniques that can be helpful to prevent a child from becoming wayward. Children need to be taught that there will be consequences for misbehavior. Parents often feel guilty about administering disciplinary action to their child, with fear that the child may react unfavorably. This unrealistic fear must be met with the words *trial and error*. Magical Mommy may need to use various discipline techniques until the child adheres to corrections administered for incorrigible or injurious behavior. Undisciplined children, who do tend to become unruly and unchecked, can ruin an otherwise peaceful home environment.

The diligent parent knows that discipline is necessary for a troubled child, one that shows tendencies that could evolve into a life of self-defeat. The shift of gears into being a teenager no longer presents crocodile tears and attention tantrums or whys, but bigger challenges seem to take hold: Your teen may tend to think they can do whatever they want and challenge your authority. Teenagers may rant "I don't care," which is a typical attitude many teens show to manipulate situations. Parents need to stay calm and not give in to a child's belligerent behavior.

How does a mommy handle a confrontational child ever dependent on Mommy and still living at home? This child is still eating the food you buy and using all the amenities (from babyhood) and resources that you have always given and that you pay for! Let me boldly say that you are not married to your child! Jacket 1 and 2 have grown into a full-blown jacket 3 nightmare when zero discipline has been applied. It is time for Mommy to put her foot down and gain control of an out-of-control situation.

Parents may want counseling themselves to gain knowledge on how to better control the situation with unreasonable and unapproachable young adults. There are child outreach programs offered in many communities for aiding parents before that bundle of joy becomes more like an eight-hundred-pound nightmare. Parenting takes a great deal of effort and fortitude.

There are so many books written on parenting, but ultimately, it is up to each parent to apply the plan of their choice to help their boy or girl become well-rounded adults in society. Nothing is magic, but knowledge about parenting is always useful!

Here is the clue:

Mommy needs to always stay calm, please! First, you must take off jacket 1. The eighteen years of wearing it must smell more than poop in a toddler's diaper! Secondly, reflect on all the time you have invested in nurturing your child. (Cry if necessary!) Realize this is not your life; rather, it is the child's life. Recognize that you will need to give your child breathing space that they can make independent choices for his or her life, regardless that they still (reluctantly) depend on you. It takes time to become an independent adult. Let go.

Magical Mommy will need to regain self-esteem to move on with her life. Take off jacket 1 and jacket 2, which you have incredibly worn eighteen years too long. At this point, jacket 3 has got to be stifling. Take it off, please! Tell yourself, "No more jackets!" And then firmly tell your young-adult child (or adult child) that you've had it with being Magical Mommy and that it is time for your child to realize he or she needs to take the responsibility to wear their own jackets. I call this jacket 4—your child's independence.

Remember, telling your child they must handle their behavior and actions is not admonishing them or meant to cause hurt but to let them know that you care about their being responsible in living. Responsibility is what being an adult is about! Magical Mommy may wait until after she has stopped crying and reflecting and has become emotionally calm to tell her children *what time of day* it is! You have invested eighteen years of your own feelings into your baby, who has grown into a young adult. You deserve respect, and your young adult needs to appreciate all your efforts in providing a safe and loving home for him or her during their growing years. It is time for your young adult to accept their own responsibility. After all, you're not Magical Mommy! You have a life too!

Now that you've taken off jackets 1, 2, and 3, you will feel the ease from parent tensions, the lighter side of yourself without wearing guilt jackets. Magical Mommy is only human, and so is your child. Both must accept significant changes that arise with the mother-and-child process that will ever be loving memories . . . in each other's life. Change can be a magical thing! (Sniffles.)

STEP VI
Dates and Time Lines

"Once upon a Magical Mommy time . . ." Now that's a perfect start to a fairy tale. Unfortunately, human life is not a fairy tale with the perfect script for a happy ending—although living happily is the perfect human aim. Human life is beset with emotions that are inherent—with dos and don'ts and what-ifs—and it's plagued by unseen obstacles that may be a harbinger of the worst fairy tale! However, happy endings in human life are possible when there is an effort to be happy.

There is a song I was taught to sing as a youngster that comes to mind: "Row, row, row your boat / gently down the stream / merrily, merrily, merrily, merrily / life is but a dream." Yet, when the stream of life seems fuzzy, it may make you dream less, especially when faced with the hurdles that one must overcome, complete with a perpetuation of many choices to experience. One of the many choices of life—rowing merrily downstream, all in its fairy-tale glory—is when Magical Mommy's teenager chooses to merrily leap into the dating game.

Let us face it, parents. Dating can be an arduous journey for any wide-eyed youngster who has been hit by the arrow of Cupid. This is the season in your child's life that he or she will be bewildered with an uphill climb and a downward spiral of emotions fit for a roller-coaster ride. Your child will struggle with their changing development to be or not to be perfect. For a young male in adolescence, he may feel like the frog in a fairy tale, who hopes that when he meets the perfect girl, a handsome prince will magically appear! Your little lady will talk excessively about her Mr. Right, until it becomes clear she is a misguided damsel with uncharted feelings that have become gnarly through her rose-colored glasses. Parents are often front and center, watching their youngsters gleaning over a potential boyfriend or girlfriend.

The worry of parents is not unusual when their child becomes mesmerized by the idea of dating, to the point that inadequacy takes hold of what used to be good old common sense. It's not easy when you see your child struggling with acne, peering in a mirror for hours, or trying the latest diets to combat what they think is a weight problem. Your child may switch their wardrobes and hairstyles and present them in an ostentatious manner to fit stereotypes they think will mask their low self-esteem. Parents need to take heed not to criticize children harshly during this fragile part of their child's growth. So it goes!

You may remember having had various self-esteem concerns as a youth and know that it is par for the individual course. Take the time to understand that when a child has weight gain or weight loss problems, they can easily become frustrated. When youngsters become overly critical of themselves, this can lead to psychological abnormalities that may become life-threatening to your child. Parents need to be watchful for unusual behavior that can prevent serious health problems, like binge eating or anorexia. With the right diet management and doctor's advice, weight balance can be achieved. Skin care problems can be managed effectively by medical advice and treatment. These problems are just a few examples, but there could be any number of personal issues young adults may have during puberty, and these need to be handled accordingly.

Parents need to respect young adults that have moved into the sexual feelings of being human, hence, they feel the need to date. Dating for your child may feel awkward, and communication with parents can be difficult. Even so, parents need to be mindful and to have open chats (friendly) with their child and with the other young adult that their child is dating or having a relationship with. This is vitally important. Let's move to the question of what position a parent enters while their young adult is involved in close interactions with another young adult, known as intimate dating. Also, how does a parent give the best instructions for their young adult to understand positive dating versus disastrous dating, and what are the best methods to garner positive results?

Firstly, parents need to recognize that discussing facts about physical intimacy with their child is an important first step. After all, your young adult still lives under your roof and by your household rules! If you are dealing with a young female, explain the role of being a lady first and then the consequences that will be incurred when she does not adhere to proper restraints. Your sweet little girl (young adult) needs to know that she is not fast food for her prospective suitors. She needs to understand that respect for herself is of the utmost importance and that she does not have to accept anything less than to be respected by young men or others.

Parents need to put in plain words to their child that respect means never being forced into doing something that makes them feel uncomfortable or afraid. If any disrespect does occur, your child will have the know-how to tell anyone "no!" Secondly, while I cannot reiterate this enough, parents have an active role in their young adult's dating habits. Let your young adult know you are always there to support them when they may be unable to deal with any situation effectively. It is no secret that many young adults can be involved in a relationship that needs parental or legal intervention.

Scheduling times for dating is an important topic to discuss with your young adult. Logic tends to fly out of the rose-colored window of your young adult's decision-making when it comes to dating. An overzealous teenager can become mesmerized by the idea of dating, to the point they can get overly distracted and are no longer concerned with time. As loving parents, gently bring your young adult back to reality. Encourage them to keep a daily routine by reminding them that their education is important and that a routine provides them with a balanced schedule to maximize time. Communicating the pros and cons to obtaining a higher education versus dating can give enlightenment to your young adult, for which they can decide how to juggle dating and educational goals. After the ground rules have been set up, parents can feel at ease—with one eye open on the ticking clock.

Most state laws have curfews that prohibit teens from hanging out past midnight. Discuss legal issues with your young adult. Explain to him or her about legal restrictions for teenagers, drinking and delinquency and the (bewitching) hours that they must abide, to avoid any serious problems with law enforcement. Dating can be a great social enhancement for your young adult, or it can bring misery and heartbreak. Mommy knows that dating is as old as you can remember—oh, do you?—and if your child knows your concerns, your expectations, the laws, and the limits, it's okay to trust them to date. However, be wise. When in doubt, let them pout!

A mother that has a teen son may need the support of his father or other male encouragement, who can jump on board to provide tips and manly advice. Young adult males need to understand how to properly handle themselves with that testosterone rocket ship and respect whom they date. Young boys who want to date need to know the legal implications for indecent behavior and actions that could be grounds for unlawful woes. Young men should be taught to take extra precautions when engaging in sexual activities and should know that the negative actions they pursue could be detrimental. Today, it is no secret that many young men are nurtured in families without a father figure. If there is no responsible male figure that can provide sound advice about dating and sex, he should be directed to literature or a church organization or group guidance counseling where he can obtain additional instructions on how to conduct himself with others, particularly when courting young counterparts and especially since *he* has taken an interest in dating!

There are so many pros and cons when young adults pursue the dating game. Although dating may be viewed by youngsters as fun, it isn't a game at all. Even if some of my readers don't share my view on this topic, most of us older folk may remember one (bad) date we experienced. It is for this reason that parents need to exemplify maturity and be the guidance for their youngsters. We are not magical parents, and for all it's worth, the best advice is this: An ounce of prevention is worth a pound of cure. I hear the midnight clock. (Zzzz . . .) Time to wake up.

Here is the clue:

Dating is normal, and it should always be discussed with your child beforehand so that they are not clueless! Dating can be fun and may result with the wonderful *L* word—*love*. (Puppy love!) Puppy love can happen, but don't get fretful yet! Let your child enjoy growing into an adult. Guidance by a loving mom or dad is the best ingredient they could ever hope for during the dating years. You are not going to be able to dictate the feelings of your young adult; therefore, it is noteworthy to be open-minded, but precaution is still needed.

Understand that your child will be leaving home at some point, and dating usually is the prerequisite to that happening. Parents should relax and remember: you love them, and your child loves you despite having found happiness in loving someone other than their parents. The time has arrived for the transition of your youngster going into their adulthood, and you have been as magical as humanly possible. It is time to let them create their own life magic. It is time to take lots of pictures with a very big Magical Mommy smile!

STEP VII
Morals and Hazards of Sex

The human life is amazingly full of excitement. It is never dull! The joys of life may seem like soaring on clouds high above, yet the waves of sorrow sometimes flow into the human heart. Be that as it may, the steady pace of living is what humans have done for centuries. There will come a time when the youth becomes aware of sexuality, and naturally, the biological senses peak. During increases of sexual productivity within the human body, this period of a human's growth cycle will take on extreme feelings that involve multifaceted decisions regarding sex.

The topic of sex is given a great deal of attention within human society around the world. The past's ideas about sex were considered a discreet subject and were socially taboo, unmentionable openly in many societies. Today, sexual anything seems common core, whether it's in TV shows, internet sites, social media, movies, and even cartoons! From the moment of birth, sex is the never-ending story for everyone. There will arise in a human's life a time that they will need to understand their physical attributes, and they must learn to control sensations that will occur with bodily changing hormones.

Life and sex are like a hand and a glove. Life can simply not exist without the sexual function. The question is simply, what is sex? The dictionary defines *sex* in multiple terms as follows:

a. *Sex* refers to a person's biological status, such as male, female, or unisex.

b. *Gender* refers to one's self-identity as a male, female, or transgender.

c. *Gender expression* refers to the way a person acts to convey their gender preference.

d. *Sexual orientation* refers to the sex of those to whom one is sexually or romantically attracted.

e. *Coming out* refers to acknowledgment of the process for one's sexual orientation.

f. *Closeted* refers to the secrecy about one's sexual orientation.

The simple subject of sex is not trivial, nor is it child's play when you start to consider the multiple categories anyone can fit. Simplicity just went out the window!

As your child developed beyond babyhood and adolescence and entered young adulthood, they most likely observed humans touching, couples openly displaying public intimacy, or loving kisses by their parents. Human affection is natural. However, there are unnatural human affections that need to be realized as they can lead to inappropriate sexual behavior and sexual abuses against minors. In cases of child violence, parental or legal action is absolutely needed! The adolescent teenager is now faced with multiple decisions in handling raging hormones that have awakened them to the mating level of their life. It is at this stage that they should be sat down and told about the hazards of sexual relations. Parents should explain that sexual feelings should be met with a sense of morality. This cannot be emphasized enough!

Parents have a duty to instruct their child about the seriousness of sexual activity without applied moral judgments. The unfortunate inappropriate actions that can result from not having moral judgment when engaging in sexual acts can be harmful to a young adult. Parents know the dangers associated with dating that could bring devastating effects due to immoral behavior, specifically sexual misconduct. Helping young adolescent teens understand the moral obligations of having a sexual relationship and taking precautionary steps will outweigh not discussing this subject. Talking over the facts of reproductive health is a sensitive matter, and the details about intercourse need to be addressed.

Mommy needs to educate her young adult about the serious health issues associated with sexual intercourse, providing abundant information about sexual diseases, or STDs (sexually transmitted diseases). There should be discussions on precautionary methods to prevent the possibility of an unwanted pregnancy. Moreover, in society today, it is common knowledge that teenagers engage in unprotected sexual activity, which is generally unknown to most parents. Of course, there are more teenagers with unwanted pregnancies (babies with babies), and sexually contracted diseases (HIV virus and others) are on the rise, according to the CDC (Centers for Disease Control and Prevention). Therefore, with the increase of concerns for sexually transmitted diseases from the national statistics data, information about safe sex must be provided by parents for the sake of their child. Buy books or CDs, or take them to see a counselor if you feel uncomfortable talking with them about the matter of intimate sexual relationships, but do something!

As parents, we're responsible for telling our children about important matters that will affect their life. Sex is how we all came to exist! Sex is not going to disappear like magic! Parents must have a discussion with their teenagers to ensure that they at least understand how to practice safe sex. Be mindful. Instill in your child the importance of the moral hazards that can come from not adhering to simple steps, such as the need for contraceptives. One barrier method to prevent impregnation of the female would be for a male to wear a condom. Various preventive methods for females are birth control medicines, intrauterine devices, or sterilization (male or female). This requires real, meaningful talk!

Finally, it will ultimately be your adolescent's decision in the end, but parents have been their child's first educator, and Mom has given her child the information to recognize the significance of practicing safe sex, having good morals, and knowing the hazards of immorality or bad decisions when having a sexual relationship. Morals are taught. This is what Magical Mommy's responsibility is about! Teach your child the dangers that can occur with promiscuity and that can lead to a future filled with dismay and unhappiness. Now that you have set the rules, laid down the facts, and given the best instructions to your teenager about the hazards of dating and sexual intimacy and what they need to be mindful and knowledgeable about, you need to let Mother Nature take its course, and let go. (You're still Mom. Monitor!) It's up to your child to follow your good moral guidance, advice, and teaching.

Here is the clue:

1. Be calm.

2. Talk lovingly.

3. Pour a cup of tea (for both).

4. Don't yell!

5. When talking becomes a senseless emotional outburst, seek professional counseling.

6. Visit the library or obtain other resources to provide informative reading material.

7. Rent or buy a video and sit with your teenager and watch together. Discuss it!

8. Be a good example. Remember, the hazards of sex can be prevented by displaying good moral behavior.

9. Understand the responsibility of sex.

10. Dating is okay.

Remember, Mommy cannot pull a rabbit out of a hat or use spy glasses to see a teenager's every move. When you provide them with reliable facts and nonjudgmental guidance, it will help give your child the advantages they need to handle sexual situations that may arise. You have done your part by open communication and giving your child relevant information during a very crucial stage in their life. You are not Magical Mommy; however, the magic is by giving genuine love and care for your child during every stage of their growth.

Cars, Licenses, and Driving

The horn is blowing, but *you* are not in the driver's seat. Or are you? You hear the whining demand, "Can I drive the car?" Oh dear, how many times must you say no! Do you eventually give in to what your youngster wants or decide that it is time to go and buy your teen a car? Let's begin to examine the hurdles parents face when their youngster wants to drive.

Firstly, driving a vehicle is serious business! The risk of an adolescent driver can be an enormous responsibility for both the parents and other people driving on the roads. Your little miss or mister begging to get behind those four wheels of what they see as fun, fun, fun must be taught the fundamentals of what driving is about. Secondly, youngsters need to be taught that there are many laws they must adhere to before they can drive a motor vehicle. The laws for safely driving on roads vary from state to state, but United States Federal Law dictates the requirements. To drive a vehicle is one thing, but to obtain a driver's license to drive a vehicle is quite another. It is considered a privilege to drive on roads in the United States.

There are many factors involved for obtaining and keeping a driver's license. To begin driving a vehicle, your child must be of the proper age of whatever state they live in. Some states will allow a child of fifteen and a half to drive with a permit. Other states require them to be at least sixteen years old. Then there is the legal requirement of motor vehicle insurance for all motorists, federally mandated, that you must obtain for a youngster to drive. Is the full picture clear yet?

Of course, there will be the licensing bureau's mandatory requirements called the driver written exam that your child must pass and the actual driver-behind-the-wheel skill test. Parents may need to pay for driving school courses to help teach their child fundamental driving skills that can help them successfully pass the Bureau of Motor Vehicles' license requirements. The driving courses that parents provide to their child can be an added expense to the family budget. Parents need to consider whether the benefits outweigh the cost and the risk of their youngster getting a driver's license. Parents can choose to avoid the costly driving schools and teach their youngster to drive. You will need to put on nerves of steel!

Mommies need to discuss the pros and cons of driving with your youngster. Driving a vehicle should not be taken lightly by an irresponsible teenager, and the emphasis must be made for the dangers of driving a vehicle, which can result in fatalities. Driving means being a conscientious and courteous driver. Another important rule to understanding driving is recognizing that you are not the only person driving! Teach your youngster about bad driving skills or mistakes that they can make while driving, which can trigger a response of road rage by other drivers. While most drivers are apt to ignore a yelling motorist that needs to express a verbal exchange for someone's driving error, it is not unusual for some motorists to become angry to the extent of verbal insults, physical threats, or dangerous driving to harm another driver. Road rage is illegal, and when this situation occurs, or *if* it does, your child needs to know how to diffuse this problem.

There are rules and *more rules* that become a part of the everyday motorist's life. Mommies must ensure that their youngster is able to manage using a car long after the driver's license has been obtained. Practice and knowledge of using an automobile make a good, skilled driver. Once all the prerequisites to driving have been satisfied, your young adult is on their way to becoming a skilled motorist on the highways and byways.

Stop! Not so fast, Mommy! What is easily gotten can *easily* be taken away! Without the correct comprehension of how important it is to follow the laws and safety rules for driving, your child could be an accident waiting to happen—a driving nightmare! There are many divisions of law enforcement that monitor motorists. There is modern technology, the watchful traffic cameras, which will take a photo snapshot of a driver's speeding vehicle or someone ignoring to stop at a red traffic signal. That can become a legal problem for a youngster if they get a citation via mail or are stopped by the flashing lights and sirens of a police cruiser.

After your child manages to pass his or her driver's requirements to obtain a driver's license, it is time for them to drive. Then you must decide whose car your child will drive. This can be the pivotal moment when mommies need to tell their young adult that it is time for him or her to secure a job to pay for the expenses of owning and using an automobile. And with driving a car, there is an abundance of responsibility. Whatever you decide, be mindful to get the right kind of insurance. Decisions! Decisions!

Explain to your child that having vehicle insurance is a legal necessity that drivers need when owning and using a vehicle. Discussions about maintaining vehicle insurance and keeping these important documents on hand within the vehicle (most often kept in the vehicle's glove box compartment) are paramount to law safety. Registration documents are legally required to be kept inside the vehicle and stickers onto the plates while driving in the United States. Accidents do occur, and a motorist without automobile insurance is breaking the law. A responsible parent will take all the necessary steps to ensure their child is safely driving on the roads. Driving is not magic, but the new exciting privilege for your youngster to take the rein in the driver's seat will be a memorable ride. It's the magic of your child growing into adulthood, thanks to Magical Mommy's steady guidance.

Here is the clue:

The beginning whines of "Can I drive?" have taken its long course with Magical Mommy talks on the responsibility of driving. Whether it is Mommy or a driving school teaching her youngster how to use a car, the hours and hours of practice, from learning to brake and manipulate the gas pedal and steering, to your child learning the dos and don'ts for driving on the roads, the day has arrived for when your child is a bona-fide driver. Now that your child has passed the grueling tests and has their driver's license in hand, Magical Mommy must decide whose car her youngster will drive. There may be the expense of buying a vehicle for your child, whether new or used, or allowing them to drive your vehicle. Maybe you have an old jalopy still in the garage, just waiting for this very day!

Get ready for the many nights without your youngster sitting on the couch, watching TV, or being secluded in their bedroom and on computer games. Your youngster may even offer to take Magical Mommy shopping. Hold on to the seat as your sweat beads begin to appear on an already wrinkled forehead. The joyride with your youngster will probably remind you of when you got your first license as you take a deep breath.

Take it all in stride, Magical Mommy, because you've made it this far. After all, you have been a gem, especially since you may need to give your car to your child to attend college. After all, Magical Mommy has been wanting a new car! Hehehe! You may not be Magical Mommy or Daddy, but you are a fantastic parent. I can hear the bells and whistles! Just keep your bonnet on and hold on to the riding magic.

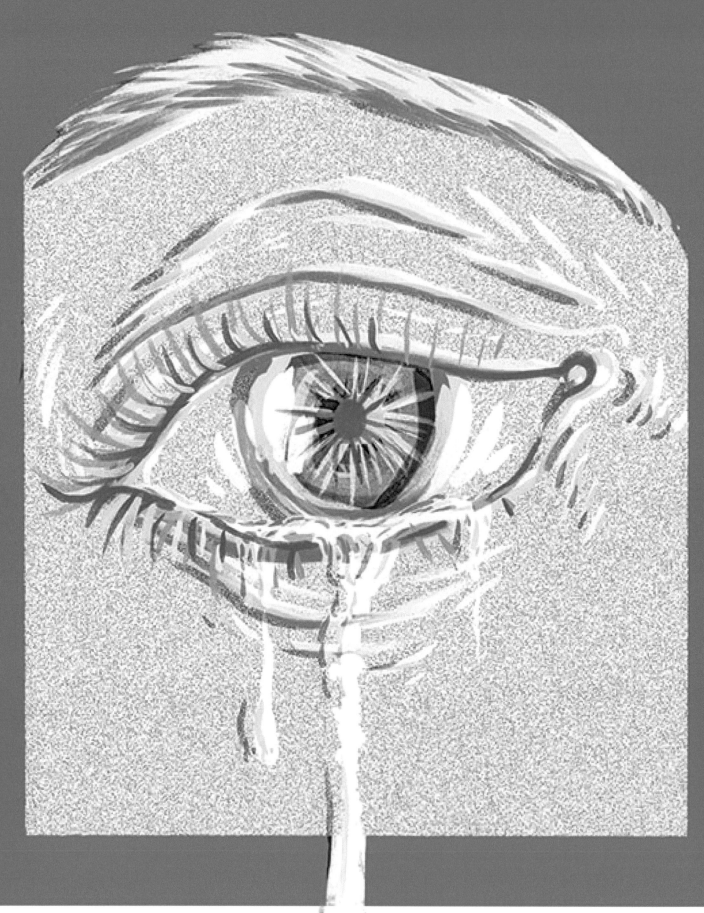

STEP IX
Tears and More Tears

There is an old saying: "Time has a way of healing wounds." Though I can agree to that saying somewhat, the gist of it is just that—time. Life is lived through it, and for us human beings, it is always full of twists and turns. The clock is ever ticking away its seconds, minutes, and hours while life moves at full speed. Moments turn into memories, and as a parent, you have gone through time guiding your children from infancy to adulthood. While there were many days that you may have been skeptical of your own abilities to teach your child the morals you believed, and you hoped that they would join the race of human success, that is not always the dream-come-true outcome.

Just when you thought you were out of the woods of having removed jackets 1, 2, and 3; made it through the dating game, sex education, and your youngster obtaining a driver's license; and proudly watched your child graduate from college and even transition into their separate lives by moving away from the nest with their dreams, that peace you finally obtained may fly out the window. *What?* you're probably thinking about now! Parents will always be . . . parents! Although your youngster had made it through all the magical steps with the grace of a dodo bird and despite all the effort and patience that you unwittingly gave to ensure your child would grow into a responsible adult, you get a call, and all you hear are sobs. *What is going on?* you ask.

Let's just say *time has a way* of giving way to more lessons when we least expect it. There comes a point in time when your adult child may need to know that you are still their supporter when they have no one else to confide in! Many parents unfortunately believe the time they weathered the storms of eighteen years with their child means that their adult siblings do not need them any longer. This type of thinking could not be further from the truth. Most every child, regardless of their age, will always have the remembrance of a mother's love. And if that adult child is still blessed to have a mother or father in their life, trust that the "jacket of love" will never be outgrown by a parent. This is a jacket Magical Mommy will wear for life! I call it MMLJ—the mommy magic life jacket!

When an adult child comes sobbing to a parent, it is generally something very major and life-changing. Parental support and guidance are again needed for crucial life circumstances that your adult child is not able to cope with alone. There are many things to consider, frustrations, or sad moods or tragedy. However, the symptoms of depression ought to be recognized. This can be due to moving beyond the nest, having relationship difficulties, employment problems, or other more serious problems. When an adult is faced with depression, this must be effectively handled without delay.

Some types of depression are as follows: major, manic, chronic, and many more. Certain types of depression may require a physician's evaluation and medicines. Major depressive disorder is a very serious medical condition of the mind and body that generally lasts longer than just a few weeks of feeling blue or sad. Chronic depression could require ongoing medical treatments and lifestyle habit changes. Manic depression, or bipolar disorder, is a serious mood disorder that causes normal moods to swing from high energy to low energy. Mania often causes sleeplessness that could last days or hallucinations and paranoid rage that will require medical treatment. The National Institutes of Health does provide a 24-7 emergency hotline for immediate medical intervention for symptoms of depression. This covers extreme anxiety, depression, and suicide prevention.

Whatever the reason that your adult son or daughter has contacted you, possibly in the middle of the night, your child needs you! Never feel that your child does not need you because they have outgrown the nest. They will always be your child no matter how old they become. Though tears are a part of life and show that we are not stone, prolonged feelings of sadness with uncontrollable crying or other abnormal symptoms can be a precursor to some form of depression. Parents should remember that we instilled the morals and values into our child that helped mold them into who they have become, responsible (or irresponsible) persons. When your adult child calls you in distress, they are reaching back for the nurturing that they feel most comfortable with—that trust in their parent.

This can be a time for recognition or reconciliation or forgiveness and handling sensitive situations that may have gone undetected by parents during a child's formative years. It is not unknown that children can or will deliberately hide their problems from an unsuspecting parent. The illness may not be known to a parent until many years later, or not at all; this is true especially for teen runaways or even for seemingly well-rounded children that have moved away from home. Parents must be ever diligent and watch their child's behavior, as odd or unusual personality changes could mean that a child may need professional help.

Life is riddled with many complexities that can affect any family, and early detection of behavior problems in children may help avoid future illness. Certain disorders that can affect a child, ranging from young children to adults, can be child bullying, cyberbullying, obesity, substance abuse, addictions, gender identity problems, anorexia, bulimia, alcoholism, drug abuse, and many more. The time may have arrived to confront overlooked problems that your adult child could have masked during their adolescence, which they need to reveal or that appeared after they moved from home.

Whatever age your child comes to you in tears is a sign of important recognition. Parents should not ignore their child when they call in tears, because this can be the crossroad between the most important decisions they are faced with making in their life. We're sensitive beings full of unpredictable emotions, and these enigmatic emotions are essential to human biological function. Mothers can become Magical Mommy in the eyes of their child, no matter the age. Mothers can give their child hope by letting them know they are always accepted and loved regardless of any problems they may be facing. Tell your adult child it's okay and that it's okay to cry! Remember to always let them know you are there for them no matter what the circumstances are, no matter how severe the issues may seem. Maybe tears can be the best remedy in moments of being emotionally overwhelmed. And when your adult child calls you in tears, be glad they did! You are there to make a world of difference for whatever ails them. They cried tears when you first gave birth (you too!), and it was Magical Mommy who nurtured her child with love. That love is always magical and is strong enough to wipe away the tears.

Here is the clue:

Hurt is a part of life. We all have felt our fair share of it, whether it was a childhood scrape on a knee, teenage puppy love, or loss of a loved one. I remember that calling home was always a great feeling, particularly hearing my mother's voice. This chapter covers the difficulty that can arise in your adult child's life. The role of any parent is to be available for your child, regardless of their age. Just remember this: Age is only the number, but love is ageless.

Let your darling child cry on your shoulders, and be a listening ear when they come to you with their worries. And always be there with empathy or sympathy or however you can help them keep hope in their life. Tears were made to fall. Parents are never able to magically make a perfect life for their child, no matter how old that child may be. Parents are not magicians, although a parent can always be there to give loving support to their children, especially when they call in tears. This is the time when Mommy can ensure she is indeed . . . magical.

STEP X
Breathe in the Air

others are the actual agent for which human life comes forth into the world. (The male benefactor is the other agent, for both male and female must procreate human life.) For centuries, the human female has been the only factor known from which humans are birthed and able to exist. There is no concrete evidence of the beginnings of mankind or how life began. There are archaeological artifacts that depict ancient civilizations throughout centuries, which have ancient stories or writings or hieroglyphics, in which it is claimed that a god or gods created the world and all that live thereupon.

The ancient civilization of Egypt reveals that human existence dates back more than five thousand years ago. However, this is an ongoing debate by archaeologists. Throughout many countries, there are extraordinary structures that were built and are the remaining evidence of humanity spanning across the globe. There have been many scientists throughout history whose theories claim that the earth was formed millions of years ago and was caused by the Big Bang theory.

With all the theories of how human life began or the question of what the purpose for human life is, all are intricately embedded, and all have been born from a mother! Mothers are the hub of humanity, and it is she who has withstood its creation for the continuation of life. Mothers birth life, and that is her part in this beautiful existence of being human. A mother has had a long ride from the moment she birthed her child. It is she who must endure the change to her biological frame for nine lengthy months. It is she who must endure agonizing pain to give birth. It is the mother who is the first protector and nurturer of the human baby.

Mothers throughout the world have been through a miraculous process, bringing the existence of the sweetest joy of life, or the saddest. Sadly, the human species is fragile, and not all human lives survive the birth process. Mothers weather the storm of life's possibilities. When a mother conceives and the child is born, she instinctively nurtures her baby. With childbearing, most mothers intrinsically respond to their child with unequivocal compassion. When her child—from a crying newborn to an inquisitive teen to an adult— has frustrations, she is there for every unexpected situation.

We mothers have been the nurturers of our children through the good times and the tough times. We have intrinsically played the role of doctor when our child was sick, the teacher to help them conquer education, the counselor for self-esteem and peer pressure, the therapist when hope seemed too far to reach, and even the role of trying to be a dad for those who didn't have a father in their life. We moms have worn so many hats, juggling so many minutes, hours, days, and years with our children, that it would put the most intriguing magician to shame. We have put on so many jackets trying to be the best mothers we can be to our children that we may have come to that point, or crossroad, in which we have been forced to ask, "What about myself?"

This is the moment that mothers must take a step back and peer into the mirror of truth and understand that she chose to have a child. This is the time that mothers ought to reevaluate their life during the stages of her child's development. Mothers should regain a sense of self and realize that the role of a mother does not mean giving up past goals, such as college education that had to be put on hold due to childbearing, or hopeful aspirations, such as becoming a writer, traveling to other countries, or other seemingly intangible desires.

We all have been the child, and all have had a mother or a father or both. Humans are born from a female, pure fact! Notwithstanding, the biological counterpart to the human equation is the human male. For without the male, humanity could not have embarked. Life is obviously caused by the female and the male. Whatever the culture, regardless of environment, whatever each must face and endure, no matter the challenges, we all had to experience the undeniable birth process and developmental stages to growing up, and . . . we made it! Many human lives around the world have had to face many life challenges, perhaps some more than others; yet people are strong and resilient, and humanity survives. Because of a mother and a father, or male and female, today you are alive and able to enjoy living life's extraordinary journey. You have the privilege of making choices for your life, regardless of your age or cultural background. And it is time to know that your child can and will make it too!

Now is the time for Magical Mommy to take the moment to breathe in the air! Burst into tears of joy if you must! (I keep boxes of tissues handy. [Sniffle!]) You have made it through waking up throughout the night to quiet a tiny baby that depended solely on you to rock away its newborn fears. You dived headlong into mastering everything from formulas to eggs, pancakes, and more to satisfy your sweet little bundle of joy! You have conquered your own fears perhaps, with hunkering down to learn new ways to help your child succeed at his education, staying up late nights to help your child pass an exam, and watching proudly when they finally reached their graduation day and walked across the stage filled with pride, knowing deep inside that it was you, their mommy, who helped make it possible for them to receive that diploma in their hand.

We moms fretted while waiting until our child waltzed through the door before the clock struck the twelve-midnight curfew chime, and we hoped and prayed the date we allowed would not become a regrettable nightmare. We can now rejoice in the fact that all the dos and don'ts we taught our teenager helped them be better equipped for becoming a responsible adult. We moms have stood the test of time by wearing guilt jackets beset for walking the plank on our child's pirate ship, of what seemed like endless emotions of their individual growth. From toddler fussiness and cuddles to adolescent depression and confidence to adult tears and understanding, Magical Mommy has worn those jackets! And most importantly, we always had our very own coat-of-arms jacket we wore with pride—the jacket of love! A mom's love for her child is priceless!

We moms have had to put ourselves in the back seat on so many occasions to give our child the things they needed to have, and we sacrificed many of our own important goals because there was never enough time to do them. Being a mom is not a part-time job! It takes endless energy and timeless effort to be a mother, and when we look back on all the years it took to give ourselves to our child unselfishly, all the time it took to groom our child into a decent human being, no matter how many faults or troubles, if we could change one thing, even that old jalopy we gave our child, we wouldn't!

It is time that mothers took a breath of air! Take a final sigh as you sit at your child's college graduation or maybe wedding, knowing you were the guiding light for them. You can now proudly watch your child put on their own jackets of adulthood. Mommy, it is now time to sip your cup of coffee and breathe in the air of relaxation because your child has taken control of their life. You have given them all the instructions you know and all the dos and don'ts and morals with which to be a responsible adult, and you have given the best years of your life to nurture them through their tears and joys. You may even be ready to enjoy a new jacket called grandmother! (Big smiles!)

Through all the ten steps within these pages, for mothers around the world, you can honestly tell yourself to feel proud. In astonishing amazement, as a mother, whether single, married, or whatever your reasons for having a child, you held the rein for eighteen years or more to support the child that you chose to birth. With all the time that you invested into your children, there is no doubt that you've been more magical than you could have ever imagined! After all, you did miraculously birth a magnificent and phenomenal human life, and it's time for you to breathe in the air of prideful satisfaction. You deserve it!

And the real clue is this:

You truly are a Magical Mommy.

Magical Mommy Resource Guide

This is a quick guide for parents seeking professional intervention.

Important Clues:

1. American Council for Drug Education, 204 Monroe St., Rockville, MD 20850

2. National AIDS Hotline, (1-800) 342-AIDS

3. National Federation of Parents for a Drug-Free Youth, 1423 N. Jefferson, Springfield, MO 65802

4. Children with Attention Deficit Disorders (CHADD), 1859 N. Pine Island Rd., Plantation, Florida 33322, (1-305) 587-3700

5. Autism Society of America, 7910 Woodmont Ave., Bethesda, MD 20814

6. National Cancer Institute, 9000 Rockville Pike, Bethesda, MD 20892, (1-800) 4-CANCER

7. National Committee for the Prevention of Child Abuse (NCPCA), 332 S. Michigan Ave., Ste. 1600, Chicago IL 60604, (1-312) 663-3520

8. VOICES in Action Inc. (Victims of Incest), PO Box 148309, Chicago, IL 60614, (1-312) 327-1500

9. Depressive Disorders (After Delivery), PO Box 1282, Morrisville, PA 19067, (1-800) 944-4773

10. National Association for Down Syndrome Hotline, 666 Broadway, New York, NY 10012, (1-800) 221-4602

11. National Association of Anorexia Nervosa and Associated Disorders, Box 7, Highland Park, IL 60035, (1-708) 831-3438

12. Epilepsy Foundation of America, 4351 Garden City Drive, Landover, MD 20785, (1-800) 332-1000

13. National Clearinghouse for Human Genetic Diseases, 2000 15th Street N., Ste. 701, Arlington, VA 22201, (1-703) 524-7802

14. Association for Children and Adults with Learning Disabilities, 4156 Library Rd., Pittsburg, PA 15234, (1-412) 341-1515

15. American Association for Marriage and Family Therapy, 1717 K Street, NW Washington, DC 20006, (1-800) 374-2638

16. National Association for Retarded Citizens, 500 E. Border St., Ste. 300, Arlington, TX 76010, (1-817) 261-6003

17. American Academy of Child and Adolescent Psychiatry, 3615 Wisconsin Ave., NW Washington, DC 20016, (1-201) 966-7300

18. National Clearing House on Marital and Date Rape, 2325 Oak St., Berkeley, CA 94708, (1-510) 524-1582

19. Youth Suicide National Center, 1824 I Street, NW, Ste. 400, Washington, DC 20006

20. Parent Support Groups—Emotions Anonymous (children ages 5–19), PO Box 4245, St. Paul, MN 55104, (1-612) 647-9712

INDEX

professional help 20, 50

puberty 17, 18, 36

R

registration documents 46

relationships 17, 19, 30, 31, 36, 42, 43, 50

responsibility 11, 13, 14, 15, 18, 19, 25,
    29, 30, 33, 43, 45, 46, 47

role model 5, 13

RTTA (response to their ability) 15

S

school 5, 10, 13, 14, 19, 20, 32, 45, 46, 47

self-esteem 17, 20, 33, 36, 54

sex 37, 41, 42, 43, 49

sexual orientation 41

sexual relationships 42, 43

substance abuse 21, 50

T

tantrums 19, 23, 24, 25, 26, 32

V

vehicle insurance 45, 46

W

weaning process 24

Printed in the United States
By Bookmasters